5/92

JN

D0793572

RALLY RACING

Sallie Stephenson

CRESTWOOD HOUSE
New York

Maxwell Macmillan Canada
Toronto

Maxwell Macmillan International
New York   Oxford   Singapore   Sydney

Copyright © 1991 by Crestwood House, Macmillan Publishing Company

Crestwood House
Macmillan Publishing Company
866 Third Avenue
New York, NY 10022

Maxwell Macmillan Canada, Inc.
1200 Eglinton Avenue East
Suite 200
Don Mills, Ontario M3C 3N1

Macmillan Publishing Company is part of the Maxwell Communication Group of Companies.

First edition

Printed in the United States of America

10   9   8   7   6   5   4   3   2   1

Stephenson, Sallie
  Rally racing / by Sallie Stephenson.—1st ed.
      p.   cm.—(Fast track)
  Includes bibliographical references and index.
  Summary: Describes the different kinds of automobile rallies, how they became popular, and what hazards, skills, and equipment are involved.
  ISBN 0-89686-694-7

  1. Automobile rallies—Juvenile literature.   [1. Automobile rallies.]
I. Title.   II. Series: Stephenson, Sallie. Fast track.
GV1029.2.S74 1991
796.7'3—dc20
                                                                91-13641

INTRODUCTION

SPOTLIGHT ON THE DRIVER

BEHIND THE SCENES

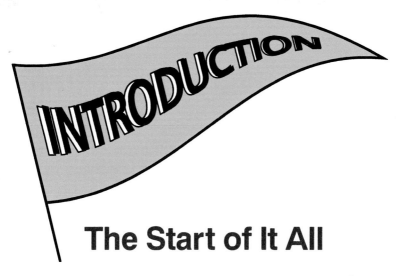

The Start of It All

Seat belt tight? Helmet fastened? Okay, now you move up to the starting position. You glance over at your partner, the **navigator** seated next to you. She will guide you through the elaborate course. The staging lights flash. Five seconds, four, three, two, one . . . Go!

You take off. Your tires churn in the sand. Your engine screams. The rear end of your car **fishtails** as you race around a corner.

You shift into second gear. You head downhill. You stay in second gear. You ease off the gas pedal. When you get to the bottom of the first hill, you pour it on! You shift into third gear and head toward another hill. The **tachometer** on your dashboard tells you the engine is running at 6,000 revolutions per minute. In third gear that's about 75 miles per hour. You downshift for a corner coming up. You narrowly miss

◀ Managing the twists and turns of a rally race requires excellent driving skills.

a water hole. There's a car on the side of the road. "Watch out!" the navigator yells. You just missed it.

In rally racing, fast reflexes are important. You have to concentrate on what you're doing. As you drive, the navigator checks the oil pressure and temperature gauges on the dash to make sure the engine is running smoothly.

You fly over the next crest. You're airborne. You land hard, then shift into second gear. The steering handles all right. You shift into third.

There is a dirt road to drive over up ahead. You power through, your foot jammed on the gas. There's only four-tenths of a mile to the next **checkpoint**.

There's your checkpoint. The navigator spots it first. At the checkpoint you'll get your next set of instructions.

Then you take off again. You're racing at full speed. Next you have to brake hard, then full throttle again.

Performance rallying is fast and exciting. You can see why it's a popular motor sport in the United States.

The Magic

Professional rally races can take place anytime and anywhere. They can be held during the day or night, in the country or in the mountains, in the desert, in the forest or alongside the ocean.

Along rally routes are special spectator stages where the public can watch the event. From there they see how the cars are running. Since there is no track in rally racing, a farmer's field or a section of a town might be blocked off for part of the rally course.

Professional rally racing may require days of difficult driving. The directions the navigator must follow are often quite baffling. Sometimes navigators need pocket calculators to figure out the time and distances of a course. Navigators

A navigator uses a light to read the directions in a rally route book during a night race.

have to work while the car flies through the course. They have to be able to write in any position. Imagine if you had to do your math homework bouncing around in a car on a rocky road. It would be hard, wouldn't it?

The navigator makes his or her calculations and records important route information on the instruction sheets, which are attached to a clipboard.

The competitors have to follow route instructions very carefully. They can be very tricky. Route instructions may be something like this:

First possible right. Maintain 40.2 miles per hour.
Turn left on first paved road.
Left at library.
Right on Long Boat Road.

An experienced rally driver can keep a car's speed very close to the specified 40.2 miles per hour. Drivers may have to maintain that speed for several miles. Meanwhile, the navigator calculates their average speed to the last decimal point. Both jobs take practice.

The navigator writes the miles traveled to the left of the route instructions. The mileage record must be very exact. After, say, two miles of driving, the instruction sheet might look something like this:

00.00   START. Mahoney's garage. Turn right.
00.56   First possible right. Maintain 40.2 miles per hour.
01.15   Turn left on first paved road.
01.89   Left at library.
01.99   Right on Long Boat Road.
02.11   Stop sign. Cross highway.

Besides recording the exact mileage from one checkpoint to another, the total mileage for the entire rally is also recorded. The goal of the rally is to arrive at checkpoints along the way at exactly the correct time.

The driver and navigator sometimes drive long distances on public roads. In professional rally racing, the route may be several hundred miles. But the course is always kept secret until the driver and navigator receive their instructions. They don't get them until just before the start of the race.

On special sections of the course the driver and navigator can run at flat-out speeds, which is as fast as the car can go. They race on both paved roads and unpaved roads that are closed to the public. The car must be fast and tough.

And the driver and navigator must be in top condition. Many of the races are held at night.

The driver does most of the physical work. But the navigator must maintain his or her concentration. If something happens such as a radiator getting punctured, the driver and navigator may have to look for water. Sometimes, even in short races, extra boots and a change of clothes are brought along.

Sometimes the rally instructions are written in the form of a **tulip diagram**, which looks just like the flower. The navigator must interpret the diagram and tell the driver what to do.

There are ten standard terms used in tulip diagrams: side road, crossroad, T, main road, straight, bear, acute, keep, left and right. These terms explain the kinds of turn. For example, if it says "bear right," the turn is slight. If it says "acute left," the driver must turn sharply.

The rally car that completes each leg, or sec-

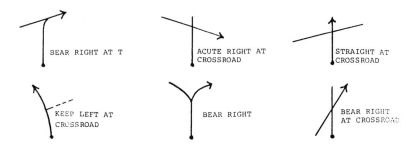

BEAR RIGHT AT T

ACUTE RIGHT AT CROSSROAD

STRAIGHT AT CROSSROAD

KEEP LEFT AT CROSSROAD

BEAR RIGHT

BEAR RIGHT AT CROSSROAD

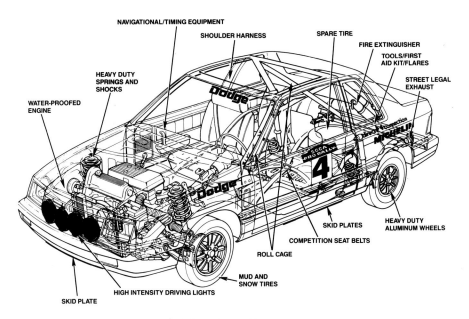

NAVIGATIONAL/TIMING EQUIPMENT

SHOULDER HARNESS

SPARE TIRE

FIRE EXTINGUISHER

TOOLS/FIRST AID KIT/FLARES

HEAVY DUTY SPRINGS AND SHOCKS

STREET LEGAL EXHAUST

WATER-PROOFED ENGINE

SKID PLATES

HEAVY DUTY ALUMINUM WHEELS

COMPETITION SEAT BELTS

ROLL CAGE

MUD AND SNOW TIRES

HIGH INTENSITY DRIVING LIGHTS

SKID PLATE

The inside of a car modified for rally racing

tion of the race between checkpoints, in the quickest time is given a zero score for that stage. In rally racing, the car with the lowest total score at the end is the winner.

Unlike most amateur rally cars, professional rally cars are highly **modified**. This means the cars are specially altered for racing. First, the car's interior is stripped. The backseat and anything else that is not necessary are removed to make the car lighter.

Lightweight aluminum may be installed to seal off the trunk from the interior of the car. A **roll bar,** or roll cage, is installed for the driver's protection in case of an accident.

Then the front seats are replaced with lightweight seats. These racing seats give the

11

driver and navigator firm support as well as comfort.

The car is fitted with heavy-duty suspension springs and shock absorbers. Special wheels and tires are installed. They have to withstand the rough surfaces on which the car will be traveling.

Professional rally cars also need high-performance engines. These engines have to withstand miles and miles of rugged, high-speed driving.

Rally cars should be quick and lightweight, yet strong enough to endure the speed and rough roads. Popular makes used in rally racing are Toyota, Audi, Mazda, Nissan, Volvo and Dodge.

These rally cars display stickers and decals that advertise their **sponsors**. The sponsors provide materials and financing for racers. Sponsors are usually manufacturers of cars, tires, shock absorbers, spark plugs and motor oil. The money they provide helps the rally teams to prepare their cars and purchase up-to-date navigation equipment.

Many sponsors put on racing events and provide prize money to rally winners. The Sports Car Club of America (SCCA) also sponsors many professional as well as amateur rallies. In 1949

▶ Cars used in rally racing are equipped with powerful engines that are able to withstand long miles of high-speed driving.

the Detroit Region of the SCCA staged the first national rally, called the Press-on-Regardless Rally.

The Press-on-Regardless Rally (POR) remains one of the most popular professional rallies today. It is held in northern Michigan in the fall. The weather conditions in Michigan at this time of year are often treacherous. Roads can be covered with snow and ice.

The course extends over 600 miles. Drivers and cars must endure the roughest roads in Michigan's Upper Peninsula.

There are six other professional, or Pro Rally, events sponsored by the SCCA. They are the Rim of the World, held in Lancaster, California; the Tiadaghton in Williamsport, Pennsylvania; the Susquehannock Trail in Wellsboro, Pennsylvania; the Ojibwe in Bemidji, Minnesota; the Gold Rush in West Cliff, Colorado; and the Coachman Stages in Olympia, Washington.

The SCCA recognizes five classes of rally cars:

1. Open Class, called the "Thunder Cars." These cars are modified factory production cars. Any alterations are permitted as long as the cars maintain the basic factory-made appearance.

2. Group A is an international class. Only limited modifications are permitted.

3. The Production Class is a popular and fast-growing class of stock cars. These cars are not

modified except to conform to SCCA safety requirements.

4. The Production GT, or Grand Touring, Class is similar to the Thunder Cars. But the cars are bigger and more powerful, like the Dodge Daytona Turbo.

5. Group N Class is similar to the unmodified Production Class, but it is also an international class. Special rules for car preparation are required.

Cars from all classes compete in a rally race, but drivers compete only against other drivers in their class.

Rally racing is a very difficult form of competition. From 50 to 80 cars compete in a rally. Less than half will finish. Few cars can last the grueling 12 to 16 hours of constant running.

There is a very unusual type of professional rally race called the Pike's Peak Auto Hillclimb. Pike's Peak is on the eastern slope of the Rocky Mountains near the city of Colorado Springs. The course is a 12.42-mile-long dirt road that ascends the 14,100-foot-high mountain. There is only one road, and it winds all the way to the top.

Drivers are alone in this rally. There is only one seat in the car. The driver who gets to the top of the mountain in the fastest time wins the rally.

At the Pike's Peak Auto Hillclimb many varieties of vehicles come to compete. There is an Open Wheel division where cars have exposed wheels and no fenders. Even large trucks compete in the Pike's Peak race.

The race to the top can be as fast as 14 minutes. But a lot of preparation goes into the event. Prior to racing, the drivers have to make practice runs to qualify for their race positions. The practice can be frustrating, especially if you have mechanical problems.

This rally is a popular event with the race crowd. These high-performance cars and trucks put on a real battle.

There are also international rally races. These races can draw big crowds and media attention as well. For example, the Monte Carlo Rally has different starting points all over Europe. Cars from as many as ten cities in Europe race toward one town. A car might start someplace on the French Riviera, on the Mediterranean coast. The top 60 or so cars are then picked for the last leg of the race, a mountain rally. But only one winner is declared.

Another exciting international rally is the East African Safari. This is a desert race where rally teams fight their way through rough roads, sand

◀ A driver climbs a trail in a mountain road race.

Winter rallies, where racers must drive on roads covered with ice and snow, provide an extra challenge.

and dust. In such conditions cars are prone to have mechanical difficulties. They may even encounter wild animals on the road.

The Shell 4000 and the Canadian Winter Rally are very popular Canadian rallies. They run in the late fall, winter and early spring. The weather conditions are often severe in these races. It can rain or snow, and the roads can quickly become slick or very muddy.

History

The first automobile rally was held in France in 1894. The course ran between Paris and

Rouen. This was not long after the automobile was first invented. Rallies in the European Alps ran through narrow mountain passes. The roads there are winding and treacherous. The constant snow made the roads a hazard even in July.

These first cars were not nearly as refined as today's cars. Drivers tried their best to keep them on the road. Mechanics would have to climb around the bouncing cars as they raced and tighten loose parts.

In time, rally races grew longer and longer. Cars became better made and faster. The events became more challenging. Long rallies held on very difficult roads became known as performance rallies.

In the United States rally racing didn't become popular until after World War II, when British sports cars were first brought to America.

The Europeans added something new to their performance rallies to make them more exciting. They added a number of **special stages** to a race. These were short but very rough sections of road, closed to the public, which tested the driver and navigator in severe conditions. These special stage sections were linked with sections of public road where racers could drive at moderate to fast speeds. But the true test came during the special stage sections. The fastest car over the special stages was declared the winner.

In the last few years professional rally racing has become very popular in the United States. Many people believe that a rally car driven at high speed is more spectacular to watch than the high-speed cars racing in the Indianapolis 500.

The North American Rally and Racing Association (NARRA) and the Sports Car Club of America (SCCA) hold major professional rallies. Drivers and navigators come from all over the United States to compete in these races.

Gimmick Rallies

Many rallies are strictly for amateur rallyists. One type of rally that everyone enjoys for the fun of it is called a gimmick rally.

A gimmick rally is one in which the rallymaster, the person who plans the rally course, uses secret tricks to confuse the drivers. The rallyists must be clever to figure out the course the rallymaster plans.

One gimmick rally, put on by the Philadelphia branch of SCCA, was called the balloon rally. A balloonist took off on a Sunday from the rally starting point. The rally drivers had to follow the balloon wherever it went. They tried, but many drivers would come to a dead end at a lake or river. Then they would have to retrace their route and find the balloon all over again.

The balloon finally came to rest on a sandbar in the middle of the Delaware River. In order to win, a driver had to swim out to the sandbar and touch the balloon.

Other gimmick rallies may involve instructions that are indirectly expressed. An instruction might read, for example: Drive at 25 miles per hour until you come to LOOHCS A.

At first you think that you may never figure out what the odd letters mean. But if you read the letters backward, you discover the key words are A SCHOOL.

In a puzzle rally, instructions can be given to you in the form of a crossword puzzle. Or, dur-

Crossing a stream is only one of the many challenges that can face a rally team during a race.

ing the race an official may hold up a card with a picture on it. For example, a picture of a baseball bat and glove may mean that the next checkpoint will be at a baseball field.

There is also the question-and-answer rally. After a number of route instructions there may be a question you have to answer. One question might be: How many signs that read DO NOT PASS do you see between Instruction Number 3 and Number 8?

In a clothespin rally a navigator may be handed a clothespin at one checkpoint. He is told he'll learn later on what it's to be used for. At the next checkpoint the clothespin is taken away and the navigator and driver are told to find their way back to where they were first handed the clothespin. So, it's important that the navigator accurately record the route taken.

If you like treasure hunts, you'll like the treasure-hunt rally where you are told to gather certain items on a list. In one rally, the last item on the list was an egg.

The winner went one step further. He got the egg and then cooked it on his radiator.

Driving the Rally Course

There are basically two types of rally courses. An open rally is one set up in the natural landscape. A closed rally race takes place on an established course, such as the Daytona International Speedway.

In an open rally course, even when the racers take practice laps, you can never know the course as well as you can a closed course—such as in circle track racing.

In stage rallies there may be more than 80 miles of course where you can travel at fast speeds. In between are the difficult staging areas. Sometimes sections of the course are traveled over and over again. But you usually don't see a particular stage area more than four or five times. And it may only be once.

Rally road surfaces are of many different types. They may be deep sand, gravel roads,

A car clears a jump as part of a rally course.

hard-packed dirt, clay, mud or a rough surface with deep ruts. In some rallies the surface is asphalt. There are all kinds of possibilities.

There is another major difference between rally racing in an open course and racing on an asphalt course. This is the weather. Since most professional rallies are on unpaved surfaces, weather conditions affect all aspects of a race. A road can change for the worse in minutes.

There are many unknown and changing factors in rally racing. A rally driver must always be ready to adapt to changing conditions.

If an experienced amateur rally driver turns professional he or she will need to get comfortable with high-performance race cars. In a 16-

hour rally comfortable seats, clothing, interior lighting and instrument layout are much more important than in the shorter amateur rallies.

Most professional rally drivers prefer to sit rather high and closer to the wheel than they would in a circle track race car. A rally driver needs better visibility to deal with changing road conditions. Sitting closer to the wheel is also less tiring over a long distance.

Rally navigators, however, generally prefer to sit lower and farther back so they have more room to make calculations and look at maps and instructions.

A new driver and navigator team may decide to obtain a map and instructions from a previous rally that used the same course. Then they

A rally team stops at a checkpoint along the route to get information about the next leg of the race.

can drive the course at moderate speeds. This helps the driver gain confidence with the car and the way it handles. And the navigator can become comfortable with the calculations he or she must make.

A good navigator is hard to find. The driver and navigator should feel confident that each can perform the assigned task. The team may, for example, consist of two friends or a husband and wife.

It is also important to have the right attitude. Your first few rallies should be just to gain experience. You can't expect to come in with the top competitors on your first or second time out.

Skills for Rally Racing

You should stick to road rallies when you first start to rally race. Avoid more complicated course rallies until you have more experience. If you decide you would like to compete at a higher level, you can volunteer to be a courseworker at a professional event. You learn a lot about rally driving just by watching.

When you drive a rally car there are all kinds of skills you have to learn. This is called **driving technique**. You have to maintain intense concentration. You need to learn to drive gracefully and efficiently. You must pay attention to every detail. This is also true for the navigator.

Most of the driving skills of performance rally racers are developed after years of practice. Once a driver has been in a few rallies, he or she begins to get a feeling for the way to handle the car on unknown roads. Some drivers call it a sixth sense. This feeling, added to good driving skills, is very important for successful rally racing.

At the amateur level rallies are less dangerous but just as much fun. These competitive games test the driver's and navigator's skills. There are straightaways and turns. There could be hidden dead ends. The races run on highways as well as on secondary roads.

At the professional level drivers and cars are tested more severely. There are sharp corners where you have to downshift and let the car slide through the turns. But the more you let the car slide, the more the car slows down. When you come out of the turn you should give your car as much gas as you can to regain your speed.

You also have to learn how to apply the brakes when cornering. One technique is called "ditch hooking." The driver hooks one of the front wheels inside a shallow ditch to help hold the car on the road. That makes it easier to control the rear end when turning. But some ditches and ruts are too rough or too deep to use.

Sometimes you may not see a corner coming up. Maybe it follows a rise in the road. You may have to guess which way the road goes. On a blind crest of a hill, the car may become airborne. But you must go over it perfectly straight. Otherwise you may break a shock absorber or hurt the suspension system or even roll the car over.

It takes quick reactions by the driver to handle a car well. You also need a fearless navigator who trusts your driving ability. Experienced car mechanics are also necessary. They maintain the car and provide roadside service during the rally.

You may be driving a rally course in the morning, in the afternoon or at night. It may go on for just a few hours or for a whole day. If it goes on for many hours you may get very tired toward the end of the race. If you are driving at night, you should have good night vision.

At what speeds will you be driving? Will the rally be made up of several legs, or driving segments, or are you going to be driving one overall run? Do you have a good navigator? Will the directions be given in terms of mileage, time,

▶ A driver's sixth sense can take him or her safely and swiftly along unknown roads.

landmarks, street names or compass readings? Will there be gimmicks?

Usually the route takes longer to drive than the time the rallymaster thinks it will take.

Hazards

Professional rally racing is particularly dangerous because it requires high-speed driving and top performance from the car and the racing team. The difficult special stage sections usually make up about one-third of the total rally course. The rally itself can vary in length from 1 to 35 miles.

Rally roads are often rough and unfamiliar. This makes driving more challenging. The course may be twisting and covered with loose gravel, clay or mud. It may be deeply rutted. The roads may run uphill. Sudden braking can cause the wheels to lock. Or the car can spin on slippery surfaces.

In the winter rally driving may be especially treacherous because of ice and snow. The road may quickly change from a perfectly dry surface to a sheet of ice.

Some clubs do not offer insurance for the rally event. They require all rally contestants to furnish proof that they are covered by their own insurance just in case an accident should occur.

Spotters at a rally checkpoint monitor the racers and make sure that everyone obeys the rules.

A Driver's Responsibilities

Organizers who plan a rally, whether it is for amateurs or professionals, insist on safe driving, especially on public roads. They expect all racers to be considerate of other drivers who use the same roads.

Sometimes there are special observation stations where rally officials check to see if the competitors are obeying the proper speed limits. There is a heavy point penalty against rallyists caught speeding on public roads.

When an open rally is being held, the local,

county and state police should be made aware of it. If a rally driver exceeds the speed limit and gets a police summons, the driver is disqualified from the rally.

Getting into Rally Racing

An amateur road rally is a good way to start rally racing. Any car can be driven as long as it is in good running condition.

Amateur rallies are like a minor league sports event. You can participate without the high costs of professional racing. Some of these amateur rallies are also called time-speed-distance, or TSD, rallies. This means that time, speed and distance are all equally important parts of the race.

A road rally usually lasts from five to seven hours. It covers anywhere from 60 to 100 miles. The object is to follow a set of instructions, which are often little more than clues.

In amateur rallying all or most of the race will be driven on public streets. The rallymaster gives out the instructions and a set of speeds to be maintained over various sections of the course. The rallymaster is the only one who knows the route the course will take. The drivers and navigators are only given clues.

From these clues, the drivers and navigators must find their way to the final destination.

Typical instructions might be: Go 2.1 miles to a school. Take a left; at 3.7 miles on your **odometer**, go down a steep hill; at the bottom, turn right at the stop sign; and so on. There may also be tricks or a puzzle to be solved.

The navigator has to keep track of the time it takes to get from one point on the route to the next. The object is to arrive at each unknown checkpoint at the exact time instructed. In addition, the driver has to drive at the exact speed listed in the instructions. He or she and the navigator also have to note the distances between certain checkpoints along the way. However, the arithmetic involved is not difficult.

There are penalties for being late to a checkpoint. If the rallymaster says that a stretch of the race should be covered in 33½ minutes, the cars should come as close as possible to that time. The team that comes closest to reaching each checkpoint and the finish in the exact time required is declared the winner. Afterward, everyone meets somewhere for fun and to relive highlights of the race.

There are usually three classes of rally racers. They are Expert, Rallyist and Novice. Novices are beginners. Some amateur rallyists simply drive "by the seat of their pants." This means

It is important to keep a rally race car in good condition. Here a mechanic checks out a car before a race.

that they guess at the average speeds and enjoy the scenery. Others use the most advanced equipment.

Navigational equipment for rally racing can range from a pencil and paper and the car's odometer to calculators and much more sophisticated instruments and gauges. The latter are mostly used by expert rallyists.

When you get to the more advanced levels of rally racing you are required to attend a professional rally driver's school before you can compete. Also to compete on a higher or professional level, your car must be modified for racing. And you will need a crew to maintain the car.

The cost for preparing a car for the SCCA Pro Rally races may run as high as $15,000. A sponsor might help you pay for some of the expenses. You will need a trailer to tow your car and some time and money to compete in today's demanding rallies.

Safety Equipment

There is no special safety gear required for amateur rally racing. But the navigator should have a digital watch and a separate stopwatch. An hour before a rally a short course is often given for those who do not know the rules. The SCCA also offers a rally school you may attend.

At the amateur level many rallies don't require technical inspections. These inspections ensure the worthiness of the car for racing. But that doesn't mean your car shouldn't be in good condition. Always check that the lights and windshield wipers are working and that the tires are in good shape. Check the ignition, brakes and exhaust system too. You don't want to needlessly break down during the rally.

If the rally takes place at night, you need to be prepared. Check your interior lights as well as your headlights. Interior lighting is essential if the navigator is to be able to read the instructions.

For professional Pro Rally racing, your car must be expertly prepared. The way a car handles depends on its size, weight, weight distribution, suspension system, center of gravity and even the shape of the body. Everything has to be considered in high-performance racing.

Mechanics at work modifying a car to compete in a rally race

To protect the navigator and driver in case of accidents, each car must have a full roll cage. Rallyists wear helmets and body harnesses that strap them into the car. They also wear fireproof driving suits. These suits are the same ones worn by professional stock car racers and drivers who compete in races such as the Indianapolis 500.

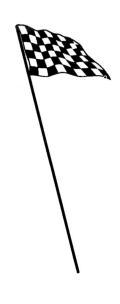

Getting Under Way

If you are serious about getting started in rally racing you should enter an amateur race. You can find one by looking in the sports pages of a newspaper or by calling a sports car dealership. Many of them sponsor rallies and can tell you when the next one will be held. You can also join the SCCA, which sponsors many amateur district and national rallies.

When you arrive, you must fill out an entry blank. The rallymaster will give you one. He or she is the person who made up the rally course. You also pay a fee to enter. The first teams to register get the lowest numbers and will start first.

The rally committee may inspect your car to be sure it is safe. Each rally has volunteers who inspect cars, help register driving teams, work at checkpoints and collect scorecards. They know about timing, scoring, communicating with driving teams and safety inspection. They make sure the rally runs smoothly.

In SCCA-sponsored races, these volunteers are licensed in their specialty. They may have been trained at weekend or evening schools. Or they may have received on-the-job training with licensed experts. These volunteers are proud of the work they do. Without them, the rallies couldn't be held.

At every rally, you are given route instructions. These guide you through the course. You and the navigator should study the route instructions before the rally begins.

The starter will let each car go at one-minute intervals. Races usually begin at one minute after the hour. If you are number three, for example, you will leave the starting line at four minutes after the hour.

During the rally, don't pay attention to what the other rally cars are doing. Rallymasters often try to confuse competitors. They may have cars going in different directions at the same time. Every car should follow its own set of instructions. The navigator should read the instructions carefully and check off each one after you complete it.

But navigation isn't all there is to successfully completing a rally. You also have to complete the route in the time the rallymaster listed in the instructions.

ATC	1	DAMITIO INSURANCE SAINT MARTIN'S	Distance	16.23 Miles	Page 3
ATC	2	ALPINE	Time	50 Minutes	Average Speed 19.5

Inst. No.	Distance Accum | Incrm		TULIP	INFORMATION	Decline Distance
1	0.00 ↓ 0.04 ↓ 0.06 0.07	0.00 ↓ 0.04 ↓ 0.02 0.01		ATC 1: SAINT MARTIN'S 1.17	16.23 ↓ 16.19 ↓ 16.17 16.16
2	0.14 ↓ 0.17 ↓ 0.18	0.07 ↓ 0.03 ↓ 0.01		1.06	16.09 ↓ 16.06 ↓ 16.05
3	0.31	0.13		!!! VERY NARROW BETWEEN POLES 0.93	15.92
4	0.50 ↓ 0.55 ↓ 0.57	0.19 ↓ 0.05 ↓ 0.02		0.67	15.73 ↓ 15.68 ↓ 15.66
5	0.84 ↓ 0.88	0.27 ↓ 0.04		0.36	15.39 ↓ 15.35
6	1.09	0.21		!! CORNER TIGHTENS UP WITH CURB ON THE OUTSIDE 0.15	15.14

Dist. Next Instr. 0.15 **Miles**

A page from a typical rally route book. The tulip diagrams tell the navigator which way the course runs.

You need to constantly check the odometer for your distance traveled. You should also check the odometer against your instructions at each checkpoint. No distances are given between checkpoints so the navigator has to compute them from the readings on the car's odometer at each point. Often you will meet other drivers at checkpoints along the course.

At each checkpoint you give your scorecard to a committee official who enters on it the car's time of arrival.

At each checkpoint you are given a new starting time. The navigator should note the exact mileage at every stop. Each checkpoint begins another leg of the race. While stopped you may also receive special clues to follow on the next leg.

WELCOME TO CHECKPOINT #4

This is what we call a BLACKJACK, a checkpoint set up just beyond an intersection where you should execute a turn. It is very easy to forget what your route instructions say when a checkpoint is seen just ahead.

Also, the turn onto Dudley Ave for Instruction 50 occurs because you pass the "DUDLEY AVE" sign before the road itself. If the sign were on the far side of the intersection, you would not have executed Instruction 50 there.

OFFICIAL MILES = 3.16   OFFICIAL TIME = 5.72

NEXT INSTRUCTION - 54   (That right turn will be onto E. Crane.)

A checkpoint clue

During the race the navigator must be able to tell the driver when to slow down or to **accelerate**. Some navigators use special tables to compute time, speed and distance. These tables are known as TSD tables. But a calculator may also be used.

Another type of checkpoint along the rally route is called a closed, or observation, checkpoint. These checkpoints are not stops, but places where courseworkers can verify that you are traveling at the right speed or that you haven't taken a shortcut.

At the end of the rally, the scorecards are totaled. You are told what your time was and what the time should have been according to the rallymaster's calculations. The car with the lowest number of points has made the fewest errors. That team is declared the winner.

The National Touring Rally

When you get to amateur national competition, the SCCA sponsors a series called the National Touring Rally. The major rally races that make up the series are the Wolf's Nose, held in Duluth, Minnesota; the Sunshine Safari in Orlando, Florida; the Trail of the Lonesome Pine in Roanoke, Virginia; the Texas Triangle and the See You Later, Alligator, both held in Houston,

A driver must decide which way to go at an intersection during a rally race.

Texas; the Chattahoochee Forest Race in Helen, Georgia; the Inaugural in Santa Clarita, California; the 100-Acre Tour in St. Louis, Missouri; the Chippewa Trail in Menomonee, Wisconsin; and the Thumbs Up in Rochester Hills, Michigan.

When you win a rally, your prize could be an emblem for your car's dashboard, a trophy or a large wall plaque. It will be something to show to your friends and relatives. Who knows, you may turn into one of the best rally drivers ever.

Good luck and good rallying.

For more information on rally racing, contact:

Grassroots Motorsports
P.O. Box 5907
Daytona Beach, FL 32118

North American Rally & Racing Association, Inc.
P.O. Box 814
Nyack, NY 10960

Sports Car Club of America (SCCA)
9033 E. Easter Place
Englewood, CO 80112
For Further Reading

The regions covered by the SCCA span the 50 states. Each region elects its own volunteer officers, holds a wide variety of automotive events in its area and has regular social and business meetings. SCCA members compete in both local divisional races and national rally races.

FOR FURTHER READING

Anderson, Eric. *Performance Rallying.* New York: Sports Car Press, 1975.

Denan, Jay. *Hot on Wheels: The Rally Scene.* Mahwah, NJ: Troll Associates, 1980.

Knudson, Richard L. *Rallying.* Minneapolis: Lerner Publications Co., 1981.

Sports Car Club of America (SCCA) Membership Guide. Englewood, CO: SCCA, 1990.

accelerate 42—To speed up.

checkpoint 6, 9, 11, 22, 33, 38, 41, 42—A place along the route where cars are timed. Checkpoints are also called controls. Some checkpoints are visible (open). At these, cars pull in and are timed when they arrive and when they leave. Other checkpoints are non-visible (closed). There, rally workers watch to be sure that the cars are driving the route properly.

driving technique 26—A racer's way of handling a car so that it performs well.

fishtails 5—A term used to describe the motion of a car when the back end slides to one side as the car corners. The car moves like a fish's tail.

modified 11, 14, 15—Changed; a car is said to be modified when it is specially altered to make it more competitive in a race.

navigator 5, 6, 7, 8, 9, 10, 12, 19, 20, 22, 25, 26, 27, 28, 32, 33, 35, 36, 37, 39, 41, 42—A person who guides a driver through a course and is practiced in that skill.

odometer 33, 34, 41—The gauge on the dashboard that shows the number of miles you have driven.

roll bar 11—A strong, tubular support structure inserted into the interior of a car to protect the occupants in case of an accident.

special stages 19, 30—Particularly difficult sections of the rally course where the car and driver are specially tested.

sponsor 12, 35—This can be a private person or a company that provides money, salaries and equipment for racing at a professional level. In return, a sponsor's products are promoted.

tachometer 5—An instrument used to measure the number of revolutions per minute of an engine. Every engine has a limit as to how fast it can turn over in each gear. The gears enable the car to move faster at the same number of revolutions per minute. The tachometer tells the driver when the engine has reached a certain limit and when, therefore, he or she must shift to a higher gear.

tulip diagram 10—A line diagram that tells a navigator which way to go at a turning point in a rally race.

Acknowledgments

I'd like to give special thanks to Tim Suddard, publisher of *Grassroots Motorsports* magazine, and J. G. Pasterjak, Jr., editorial assistant at *Grassroots Motorsports*, for helping in the research of this book.